THE "FAITH IN ACTION" SERIES

General Editors: Geoffrey Hanks and David Wallington

FRIEND OF DRUG ADDICTS

THE STORY OF DAVID WILKERSON

R. J. Owen

GW00703115

RELIGIOUS AND MORAL EDUCATION PRESS

Religious and Moral Education Press
An imprint of Chansitor Publications Ltd
A Subsidiary Company of Hymns Ancient & Modern Ltd
St Mary's Works, St Mary's Plain
Norwich, Norfolk NR3 3BH

All the photographs in this book are reproduced by courtesy of Bob Combs.

Cover photograph by courtesy of Pictor Ltd.

First published 1974
Reprinted 1975, 1978, 1980 (with revisions), 1982, 1984
Reprinted 1993, 1994

Printed in Great Britain by BPC Wheatons Ltd, Hennock Road, Exeter

ISBN 1 85175 015 0

FRIEND OF DRUG ADDICTS

The story of David Wilkerson

Seven boys were on trial for murder. They were all teenagers and members of a gang called the Dragons. They had brutally attacked and killed a fifteen-year-old polio victim called Michael Farmer. The seven of them had stabbed Michael in the back with their knives and beaten him over the head with studded belts. This happened in New York.

Reading an account of the boys' trial, David Wilkerson felt a strong urge to help them. David was the minister of a small Pentecostal church in Philipsburg, a country village a long way off in Pennsylvania, another part of the United States of America.

It was in 1958 that David travelled the 350 miles or so from Philipsburg to New York, in order to be present at the final stages of the boys' trial. Yet he seemed to achieve nothing. His attempt to speak to the judge, as he was leaving the court one day, resulted merely in his being thrown out by the courtroom guards. He was then questioned by the police and interviewed and photographed by press reporters. In the newspapers he was pictured as a 'crank'—a wild-eyed, Bible-waving country clergyman, who had interrupted a murder trial.

He returned to Philipsburg, feeling sad and ashamed.

"Hey, Dave"

Yet the idea of helping the seven boys on trial kept nagging
David. It was not long before he travelled to New York
again. As he neared the city centre, he suddenly had the
strong feeling that he ought to get out of his car. He stopped
at the nearest empty parking-meter and got out.

He had only walked a few yards when he heard a voice
shouting, "Hey, Dave!" He turned round. Leaning
against the side of a building, and beneath a sign saying
"No Loitering. Police Take Notice", were six teenagers.
All but one of them were smoking, and all looked bored. A
seventh boy had separated himself from the group and came
up to David.

"Aren't you the preacher they kicked out of the Michael
Farmer trial?" the boy asked. "I'm Tommy. I'm the
leader of the Rebels." Tommy introduced David to the
other members of the gang. One by one the boys left the
side of the building and came up to meet David. Only one
of them did not move.

It was several minutes later, while David and the boys
were chatting, that he eventually went up to David.
"Davie," he said. Then there was a pause. Very deliberately
he ran his knife-blade down the buttons of David's coat,
flicking them one by one.

"Davie," he said at last, "you're all right. But Davie, if
you ever turn on boys in this town . . ." David felt the
knife being pressed lightly against his stomach. He under-
stood the warning.

David had made his first contact with a teenage gang.
Now he was determined to see the seven imprisoned boys
whose trial had first brought him to New York.

Finding Luis Alvarez

There were two ways, and two ways only, by which David could gain entry into the prison to see the boys. One was to have the judge's permission, which was unlikely because of the earlier incident. The other was to get the written permission of each parent, but the police refused to give David the addresses of the boys' homes.

The leader of the gang responsible for the murder of Michael Farmer was Luis Alvarez. The name 'Alvarez' is Spanish, but it is common in New York and David's attempts to phone the hundreds of Alvarezes in the telephone directory met with no success. It was a waste of time and a waste of money.

Sitting in his car, David prayed. "Lord," he said, "if I'm here on your errand, You must guide me. I've reached the limit of my ideas. Lead me where I must go."

David then drove the car off, having no idea where he was heading. He got caught in a stream of traffic and eventually found himself in an area of New York called Spanish Harlem. Suddenly, he felt a strong urge to get out of the car, just as he had once before. Again, he drove into the first available parking space.

Near where he parked his car sat a young Negro boy. David asked him if he knew where Luis Alvarez lived. The boy's reply was staggering. "Man," he muttered, "you parked right in front of his house!"

So David received Mr Alvarez's permission to visit his son in prison. On his way down the steps from the house, David nearly bumped into a young man of about seventeen. The fellow looked at him. "Aren't you the guy who was thrown out of Luis' trial?" he asked.

The boy thrust out his hand, saying, "I'm Angelo Morales, Rev'run. I'm in Luis' gang."

Angelo took David to the parents of the other imprisoned

Steps of a tenement house in Greenwich Village, New York

boys and they all gave their permission. Unfortunately, it was at the prison itself that an unexpected difficulty prevented David from meeting the boys. The prison chaplain, who had the boys in his care, declared that in his opinion it might have a disturbing effect on the boys to meet a stranger. His opinion was respected. Disappointed, David returned to Philipsburg.

Shortly afterwards, the seven Dragons on trial for murder were sentenced. Four were found guilty and sent to prison. One was sent for treatment at a mental hospital. David had failed to contact any of these boys and yet he remained convinced that God had a purpose in all this. Perhaps he was meant to help other teenagers in New York.

New York
For the next four months, David went to the city once each week and walked around the slum areas where teenage

gangs lived. It was during this time that he first learnt of the violent fighting, sex parties and drug addiction which went on in these areas. He also had some amazing experiences as well. On one occasion, after he had talked about Jesus Christ and God's power to change lives, the four leaders of one of the most feared gangs in New York knelt down to pray in the street, in front of a crowd of onlookers. All four became Christians.

Another gang leader who became a Christian during these months was called Israel. He was fascinated with the Old Testament stories.

"I'm in the Bible!" he said to David, "Look, here's my name all over the place!"

David was thrilled to see the change in the lives of so many young gangsters. In fact, already, two former gang leaders were training to become Church ministers. Yet in the spring of 1959 came news which horrified David. Israel was in prison for murder.

For several months Israel had given up his former way of life with the gang. He had done all he could to live honestly and peacefully. But then he was 'drafted' into a gang. When gangs are just starting, or when their numbers are low, any boy in the neighbourhood can be 'drafted'. This means he is *forced* to join a gang. He is stopped in the street and told that from that moment he is a gang member. He is expected to obey all gang orders and take part in gang warfare. If he refuses, a beating follows. If he still refuses, his thumbs or an arm are broken. If he continues to refuse, his life is threatened.

Israel was shot at several times before he returned to the gang life. Soon after he agreed to being 'drafted', he was involved in a gang fight in which one boy was killed. He did not commit the murder himself, but he was found guilty with others of being responsible for the death.

A gangland warning

This sad news caused David to realize that he had to do more than just preach to the lads. He ought to be at hand to help them when problems cropped up, as they began to try to change their way of life.

God speaks

One Wednesday in August 1959, after an evening meeting at his country church, David went outside. The moon was shining with an unusual brightness, and it seemed to light up a large field of wheat. David remembered what Jesus had said about fields of wheat: "Look round on the fields; they are already white, ripe for harvest." He imagined that each of the blades of wheat was a young person on the

7

streets of New York. Then he looked at his country church. As he looked, it seemed as if a quiet inner voice spoke to him, as clearly as if a friend had been standing nearby: "The church is no longer yours. You are to leave." David felt that these words in his mind came from God. It was God talking to him. He decided to obey. He left the church.

The following winter, David began full-time work among teenagers in American cities. A large house in Brooklyn, New York, was bought and decorated through money given by friends and people interested in youth work. The house, renamed 'Teen Challenge Centre' became the home for boys and girls who needed special help. The idea was that they would be able to live in an atmosphere of love and discipline. They would learn to overcome their drug addiction, sexual problem or whatever was at the root of their trouble. They would be given a chance to realize the help and happiness of being a Christian.

Enemies

One of the young men who worked with David at the Centre was called Carlos. He had been a member of one of the worst fighting gangs in New York—the Suicides. One day, he decided to find his former gang and tell them about his Christian faith.

"I hear you got religion," sneered the leader of the Suicides. "I hear you won't fight no more."

"That's right," replied Carlos.

The leader of the Suicides pulled out a knife. "You'll fight if I stab you," he shouted.

Years of experience had taught Carlos that this threat was real. He jumped sideways and ripped off a wireless aerial from a nearby car. The aerial made a good weapon

in such an emergency. Then, suddenly, Carlos changed his mind. He broke the aerial across his knee and threw it to the ground.

"No, I'm not going to fight," he said quietly.

The leader of the Suicides stepped forward and rammed his knife deep into Carlos' ribs. The Suicides walked away and ignored the wounded young man's cries for help. When Carlos was eventually taken to hospital, it was touch-and-go whether he would live. Fortunately, he did survive, but not without much suffering. This is what happened to just one person who helped David. Others had similar experiences.

Success and failure

Despite such opposition, David and about twenty helpers did what they could for teenagers in trouble. Many of the young people were drug addicts. After staying at Teen Challenge Centre some were cured of their addiction. Others, unhappily, remained 'hooked'. One of these was a boy called Joe.

Joe was a likeable fellow, tall and athletic. He had been on heroin, one of the worst drugs, for over eight months before going to the Centre. Immediately, Joe went through 'cold turkey', which is sudden, complete withdrawal from drugs. It has been said that 'cold turkey' is the nearest thing to hell on earth. About two hours after the effect of the previous dose of the drug has worn off, 'withdrawal symptoms' are experienced. First, there is a deep craving for another dose, a craving which makes the person nervous, ill at ease and unhappy. Then the addict begins to sweat. Painful stomach cramp grips him. He starts to be sick and retches for hours on end. He feels sharp pains all over. He imagines things, more horrible than any

10

David Wilkerson

nightmare. Usually, this goes on for three days and nights without a break.

Such was the case with Joe. On the fourth day he felt better and, smiling and seemingly thankful, he left the Centre. The following morning news came that Joe had been arrested, charged with robbery and possession of drugs. So sometimes David met with failure as well as success.

Girls as well as boys were helped at the Centre. Elaine, for instance, was a teenage girl gangster. She was a hard girl, filled with hate. She was a discipline problem at school and at home. She went to wild parties which ended in drunkenness and sexual immorality. Through living at the Centre, Elaine learnt a happier way of life. She learnt to respond to care and love, and to trust in and care for others. She stopped going to wild parties, and found greater satisfaction and enjoyment in her new life.

There was more success than failure. During the first six months of the Centre's existence, over 2500 young people came to know Jesus Christ through David's work. From being drug addicts they had become free and clean. From being drop-outs they had become young people with a new outlook and a purpose in life. From being criminals and behaving immorally they had become active citizens with something to give.

David in Britain

Besides his work in the United States, David has also travelled throughout Europe. He has talked to teenagers of different nationalities, seeking to help them and show them what being a Christian really means.

One thing David discovered was that most teenagers of all countries had rejected the Church. For example, of two

Teen Challenge Centre

hundred teenagers he met in Bristol, not one had been to church for five years. They thought the Church was for kids, old women and 'softies'. Typical of the comments David heard were: "The Church doesn't mean anything to me any more", "Our minister just doesn't get through to us," and "The Church leaves me cold about God".

Sometimes, though, David found that young people only said these things to cover up the real reason. Too many teenagers are afraid that being a Christian would cut down their enjoyment of life. David's message to young people is that this idea is quite wrong. He admits that anyone who wants to be a Christian must be willing to give up bad habits and wrong behaviour. On the other hand, that does not mean being a killjoy. Also, in return, the Christian receives forgiveness of sin. He is no longer afraid, because he believes that God cares for him and will watch over him. He finds that prayer works and is a tremendous help in trouble. He experiences the reality of a friend whom he can always rely on—Jesus Christ. In short, says David, becoming a Christian does not solve all our little troubles, but it brings real, satisfying happiness and inner peace.

David has often been accused of over-simplifying teenage problems and their solution because he preaches a simple message of faith in Jesus Christ.

"But," comments David, "no one can deny it works."

Nicky Cruz, one-time leader of another New York gang called the Mau Mau, who first welcomed David with a slap, a spit and a "Go to hell!", is now a Church minister working amongst young people. This case is typical of many young people David has helped.

There are now as many as 116 centres in other towns like the Teen Challenge Centre at Brooklyn, New York. David keeps in contact with each one, although, as he is so busy telling teenagers about Jesus Christ and trying to interest older people in the work he is doing, he does not spend as much time at the centres as he would like.

Drug addicts continue to be cured. In fact, seventy-five per cent of the young people who go through 'cold turkey' at the centres stay free of drugs afterwards. Teenage thieves and prostitutes continue to give up their ways of earning easy money and instead live decent lives. All this because they have come into contact with a Teen Challenge Centre. All this as a result of David Wilkerson's one-man mission to New York in 1958.

BIOGRAPHICAL NOTES

David Wilkerson was born in Hammond, Indiana, in the United States of America, in the mid 1930s. He was the eldest son of a family of five born to a Pentecostal minister and his wife. On leaving school, David attended Central College in Springfield, Missouri, for a year before entering the ministry. In 1952 he married and later had four children – Debbie, Bonnie, Gary and Greg. For five years he was the pastor of a small Assemblies of God church, until in 1959 he became a full-time worker among the teenage gangs of New York. The first Teen Challenge Centre was opened in Brooklyn in the spring of 1961. David has travelled extensively and written numerous books. His best-seller, *The Cross and the Switchblade*, first published in 1962, has sold more than 12 million copies and has been made into a film with the same name.

In 1970 David handed over responsibility for the Teen Challenge Centre in Brooklyn to his brother, Don, and became an itinerant preacher. In the following year he set up World Challenge Incorporated to organise his meetings and crusades. In 1976 he set up the Twin Oaks Leadership Academy near Lindale, Texas, to train young people for the Christian ministry.

THINGS TO DO

A Test yourself

Here are some short questions. See if you can remember the answers from what you have read. Then write them down in a few words.

1 In which part of America was David Wilkerson a minister at first?
2 Who was the first gang leader that David Wilkerson met?
3 Which part of New York did Luis Alvarez live in?
4 Who stopped David Wilkerson from visiting the boys in prison?
5 Why did Israel join another gang?
6 How did David Wilkerson know he had to leave his country church?
7 Why did Carlos refuse to fight the leader of the Suicides?
8 What does it mean if a drug addict goes through 'cold turkey'?
9 What was the name of the New York gang leader who became a Church minister?
10 How many other 'Teen Challenge Centres' are there now?

B Think through

These questions need longer answers. Think about them, and try to write two or three sentences in answer to each one. You may look up the story again to help you.

1 Why did David Wilkerson want to help boys who were murderers?
2 How did God use the failure of the first visit to New York to show David Wilkerson his new work?
3 How did David Wilkerson find the house of Luis Alvarez?
4 How does David Wilkerson help the young people who go to the Teen Challenge Centre?
5 Why do you think people like Carlos want to tell their old gang friends about Jesus Christ, when they sometimes get hurt doing it?

18

6 "If you are a Christian you have to give up all the fun in life". What does David Wilkerson reply to people who say this?

7 Look up St Paul's *Letter to the Romans* 1, verses 28–32. Which of the words in these verses apply to the gangs in New York? Do these verses apply to young people in our own country today? (Give reasons.) Read *Romans* 7, verses 24–25 for Paul's answer to the problem.

C To talk about

Here are some questions for you to talk about with each other. Try to give reasons for what you say or think. Try to find out all the different opinions which people have about each question.

1 Do you believe that taking drugs makes people happier? Is drug-taking a harmless kind of amusement? Why do some people become drug addicts?

2 Why is it that David Wilkerson and the Teen Challenge Centres are so successful in curing drug addicts? Does religion really help, or is it just another kind of 'escape'?

3 Is it possible for people to change suddenly from a bad way of life? What made the gang leaders kneel down and pray?

4 Is it possible for God to 'guide' people? How do you explain David Wilkerson's feeling 'a strong urge' to do things like going to New York? Do you know of any other people who claim that God has guided them?

5 Can God 'speak' to people? Compare David Wilkerson's experience with that of Abraham in *Genesis* 12, verses 1–3. How do you explain it? Can it happen to people today?

D Find out

Choose one or two of the subjects below and find out all you can about them. You will find books such as an atlas, a dictionary and an encyclopaedia very useful. Your school geography books may also help. Sometimes you can find interesting pieces in newspapers which you can cut out. You may find books about some of these subjects in your school or public library.

1 *The U.S.A.* Draw a map of the U.S.A. and mark the city of New York and the State of Pennsylvania. How many people live in New York? Who founded Pennsylvania? Cut out any pictures you can find of New York.

2 *Gangs* Why do young people join gangs? Are all gangs bad? What makes some gangs do terrible things such as fighting and murder? Why are there so many gangs in the part of New York called Harlem? What can be done to stop these gangs fighting and killing each other?

3 *Crime* Find out the figures for different kinds of crime in this country or in America. Are crimes increasing or decreasing? What should be done to people who commit murder?

4 *Drugs* Collect newspaper cuttings about drugs. What happens to people who take drugs? Why do you think they take them? Find out about the work of the 'New Life Foundation'.

5 *The Pentecostal Church* What unusual things do members of this Church believe? Why is it called the 'Pentecostal' Church? Do you think that the passage in the Bible, the Acts of the Apostles chapter 2, has anything to do with the name?

USEFUL INFORMATION

Addresses

Teen Challenge (U.K.)
16 Highfield Drive
Carlton
Nottingham NG4 1JQ.

New Life Foundation Trust
The Red House
Kelham
Newark
Notts NG23 5QP.

Institute for the Study of Drug Dependence
1–4 Hatton Place
Hatton Gardens
London EC1N 8NT.

N.B. Remember to enclose a stamped, addressed envelope for the reply. A postal order for 50p would also be helpful, if you want plenty of material.

More books to read

Beyond the Cross and the Switchblade, by David Wilkerson (Hodder & Stoughton) (T).
City of Darkness, by Geoffrey Hanks (R.M.E.P.) (P).
The Cross and the Switchblade, by David Wilkerson (Marshall, Morgan & Scott, Hodder & Stoughton) (T).
Drug Takers, by John Foster (Edward Arnold) (P).
The Gangster Who Cried, by Roger Owen (R.M.E.P.) (P).
Hellbound, by Don Wilkerson (Anfield Music Ltd) (T/P).
The Pentecostal Churches, by Krister Ottosson (R.M.E.P.) (P).

(T) = suitable for teachers and older pupils
(P) = suitable for younger pupils

Films

The Cross and the Switchblade (115 min), colour. Shows the work of David Wilkerson. Available for hire (and for sale in Betamax and VHS video format) from the National Film Crusade, P.O. Box 4, Bristol BS99 7SA.
The Drug Takers (20 min), colour. From the Independent Television for Schools series, *The Facts Are These*, available to buy or hire from Concord Films Council Ltd, 201 Felixstowe Road, Ipswich, Suffolk IP3 9BJ.

Filmstrip

Facts about Hard Drugs   Available from Educational Productions Ltd, Bradford Road, East Ardsley, Wakefield, W. Yorkshire WF3 2JN.

Teaching Pack

Free to Choose   Teacher's notes and ten pupils' units of work on drugs, produced on plastic card for photocopying. Available from TACADE, 2 Mount Street, Manchester M2 5NG.